THE MOVIE INDUSTRY

GLOBAL CITIZENS: MODERN MEDIA

Published in the United States of America by Cherry Lake Publishing
Ann Arbor, Michigan
www.cherrylakepublishing.com

Content Adviser: Jessica Haag, MA, Communication and Media Studies
Reading Adviser: Cecilia Minden, PhD, Literacy expert and children's author

Photo Credits: ©Stock-Asso/Shutterstock.com, Cover, 1; ©Serge Ka/Shutterstock.com, 5; ©Everett Collection/
Shutterstock.com, 6, 7, 9; Jack Long/National Film Board of Canada. Photothèque/Library and Archives
Canada/PA-169509, 8; ©Jean-Pierre Dalbera/flickr.com, 10; ©Tupungato/Shutterstock.com, 13; From *The
Tale of Genji* (1951)/Public Domain/Wikimedia Commons, 14; ©Andrey Khachatryan/Shutterstock.com, 15;
Postcard of Gaumond Palace/Taken in 1914/Public Domain/Wikimedia Commons, 16; ©Mikkelvog53/
Shutterstock.com, 19; ©RukiMedia/Shutterstock.com, 20; ©antb/Shutterstock.com, 22; ©Andrea Raffin/
Shutterstock.com, 25; ©Tanase Sorin Photographer/Shutterstock.com, 26; ©Serge Ka/Shutterstock.com, 27;
©Serhii Bobyk/Shutterstock.com, 28

Library of Congress Cataloging-in-Publication Data has been filed and is available at catalog.loc.gov

Cherry Lake Publishing would like to acknowledge the work of the Partnership for 21st Century Learning.
Please visit *www.p21.org* for more information.

Printed in the United States of America
Corporate Graphics

ABOUT THE AUTHOR

Wil Mara has been an author for over 30 years and has written more than 100 educational titles
for children. His books have been translated into more than a dozen languages and won numerous
awards. He also sits on the executive committee for the New Jersey affiliate of the United States
Library of Congress. You can find out more about Wil and his work at www.wilmara.com.

TABLE OF CONTENTS

CHAPTER 1
History:
Movies—Yesterday and Today 4

CHAPTER 2
Geography:
Movies Around the World 12

CHAPTER 3
Civics:
The Workings of a Movie 18

CHAPTER 4
Economics:
The Numbers Behind the Films 24

THINK ABOUT IT.. 30
FOR MORE INFORMATION.................................. 31
GLOSSARY 32
INDEX 32

History: Movies–Yesterday and Today

People have been communicating with each other for thousands of years. What began as rock carvings has slowly changed into books, newspapers, magazines, movies, radio, TV, and the Internet. Together, they are called **media**.

The movie industry plays a valuable role in society. Movies like big summer **blockbusters** can entertain people. **Documentaries** can educate people. Movies can use important themes to deliver timely messages that change the way we think.

Movies during the late 1800s to early 1900s were called "moving pictures" or "photo plays."

Once Upon a Time

The movie business began in the 1890s, not long after the invention of the Kinetograph. This was the first workable movie camera. There were many limitations to camera technology back then. Films had no sound, the images were in black and white, and they were only about a minute in length. By 1910, there were about 9,000 theaters across the United States, and movies

Metro-Goldwyn-Mayer (MGM) used several real lions to photograph and film their logo over the years, starting with Slats in 1917.

were about 10 minutes long. Most of the major films in the United States were being made in the Los Angeles, California, neighborhood of Hollywood.

By the 1920s, some movies had already been made in color. The first major motion pictures to use color technology, or **Technicolor**, were *The Wizard of Oz* (1939) and *Gone with the Wind* (1939). *Gone with the Wind* became so popular that it earned more money over time than any other movie in history. To date, it has earned about $3.5 billion!

Before advancements in technology, movies did everything by hand, from building sets to physically cutting and splicing film in order to edit.

In the past, animated films were hand-drawn.
Today, they're animated on the computer.

Ups and Downs

With the rise of television in the 1950s, the film industry lost some of its popularity. By the 1960s, films were being made in other countries, in competition with Hollywood. However, in the late 1970s and the 1980s, the American movie business benefitted from the rise of young and talented **directors**. Steven Spielberg and George Lucas were two of them. They alone made some of the biggest blockbusters of the time, including *Jaws* (1975), *E.T. the Extra-Terrestrial* (1982), and the *Star Wars* (1977–2005)

The first drive-in theater opened in 1933 in Camden, New Jersey.

Motion capture suits record an actor's movements.
This helps in creating digital characters.

and *Indiana Jones* (1981–2008) series. The first *Star Wars* movie by itself has earned about $1.5 billion to date.

The Digital Age

The 21st century has ushered in a highly **technological** era in the movie business. Filmmakers used to build expensive sets, create elaborate costumes, and rely on a **special effects** team. Now, more and more of them are leaning toward **computer-generated imagery** (CGI). CGI allows filmmakers to create out-of-this-world movies without paying out-of-this-world prices. For the most part, building a fictional world on a computer screen is far less expensive than building one in real life.

Developing Questions

CGI and other technologies allow filmmakers to create alternate realities more convincingly than ever before. While this might sound great for the average movie fan, some people complain about CGI. Use the Internet and your local library to research this topic further. What do you think these complaints might be? What other potential problems do you see with the use of CGI?

CHAPTER 2

Geography: Movies Around the World

The movie industry produces thousands of films a year. In 2017, **revenue** from movies totaled more than $41 billion. The United States continues to be number one in the movie market. But it's not just Hollywood making these movies. Other countries have seen an increase in movie production and are making an impact.

United States

Before Hollywood, New Jersey was the center of the film industry in the United States. But because of strict regulations in that state, filmmakers fled to the Hollywood area. The movies

Created in 1923, the Hollywood Sign originally spelled out "Hollywoodland" and was used as an advertisement for a real estate company.

made then were inspired by the war being fought in the early 20th century. Themes of heroism, secrecy, and wartime effort were common, and many films served as **political propaganda**.

Hollywood continues to be the oldest and most influential **producer** of movies in the industry. On average, the United States releases 600 to 700 feature films a year, with an average production budget of over $60 million. While Hollywood produces the world's **top-grossing** films, it doesn't produce the most films.

Japan has been making movies since 1897.

India

India's "Hollywood" is called Bollywood. People were making films in India as far back as 1899. By the 1930s, Indian filmmakers were keeping up with the United States, producing about 200 films each year. Today, the heart of the Indian film business is found in the city of Mumbai, located on the nation's western shore. In 2017, the Indian industry produced nearly 2,000 films. That's more than twice that of the United States and more than any other country in the world!

[21ST CENTURY SKILLS LIBRARY]

The word "Bollywood" was created in the 1970s.

France dominated the movie industry until World War I (1914–1918).

China

Like India, China has a long history in the film business. The first Chinese film was made in 1905. It showed a performance of a popular Chinese opera. Today, many Chinese films are earning good reviews, winning awards, and making money at the **box office**. In 2017, China produced nearly 1,000 films—more than the United States. Many sources predict that by 2020, China will pass the United States as the largest movie market in the world—both in terms of the amount of blockbusters produced and the number of people watching movies on the big screen.

Gathering and Evaluating Sources

While Hollywood has been the filmmaking capital of the world for decades, other nations are clearly in the running. Experts believe that China will soon take that number-one spot. Why do you think this is? Use the data you find from the Internet and resources found at your local library to support your answer.

CHAPTER 3

Civics: The Workings of a Movie

The road to making a movie can be a long one. The movie industry has many working parts and employs thousands of people. In the United States alone, more than 350,000 employees earn their living making movies.

Every movie that has ever been made has started the same way. Someone has an idea. This idea is turned into a **script**, which is presented to someone in the industry who has the power to move it forward. That person might be a director, producer, or actor. These people know if the potential movie will be **profitable**.

Movies use clapperboards as markers to help sync the sound and motion when editing.

Some movies cost a lot to make. The last movie in the *Harry Potter* series, *Deathly Hallows: Part 2*, cost about $125 million to produce. But it earned over $1.3 billion worldwide. Other movies can be produced cheaply and still make a huge profit. The 2004 cult comedy *Napoleon Dynamite* was filmed for only $400,000 but earned over $46 million!

Pre-Production and the Shoot

Before filming can begin, there is an entire process that happens. This preparation time can take months. The film is planned out,

Shooting on location can be cheaper than building a set in a studio, but there is a lack of control, from the weather to the sound.

usually through **storyboarding. Screenwriters** write the script. Schedules are made. Necessary equipment is rented. **Location scouts** look for budget-friendly places to film if it won't be done entirely in a **studio**. Actors are cast. Rehearsals are run. Costume designers, the art director, and production designers are among the many who work with the director and producer to bring the script to life. All this plus more goes into the makings of a movie well before the filming process.

The **shoot** can last months. On average, it takes about 3 months to shoot a studio production, but it can take longer if the shooting location changes. Some locations are more movie-friendly than others. Because of strict regulations in the past, many Hollywood-produced movies have been filmed outside the United States. However, several states have attempted to bring filmmakers back by offering tax **incentives** called movie production incentives (MPIs).

States offer MPIs to boost their local economy. A film production can have hundreds or thousands of crew members. This means hundreds or thousands of people will be staying, eating, and buying things in the state. For example, *Iron Man 3* (2013) had 3,310 people working on the movie!

The film score, or the background music in a movie, usually helps set the mood in a movie.

Post-Production

Once the shoot is completed, post-production begins. This is usually when special effects are added and the movie's **sound track** is composed, performed, and recorded. Thanks to advanced technology, many errors can be fixed fairly easily. If an actor's **dialogue** wasn't recorded clearly, the actor can go to a studio and **dub** over it. Sometimes actors need to reshoot a scene. Average post-production time is about 6 months.

Distribution

Once a film has been completed, the company in charge of the studio gets to work. It arranges with **distributors** to get the movie into theaters. It also begins a **marketing campaign** to get people excited about seeing it.

Developing Claims and Using Evidence

CGI technology has allowed filmmakers to create amazing worlds, characters, and special effects without breaking the budget. While CGI can save a lot of money, there is still an enormous amount of time, creativity, and effort involved. For example, Life of Pi (2012) is only 15 percent real. The rest was done using CGI. It took an entire year just to create computerized hairs on the CGI tiger! Overall, the movie took about 4 years to make. Knowing how long it takes to create CGI effects, do you think it's worth the effort? Why or why not? Research the topic further and use the data you find to support your answer.

Economics: The Numbers Behind the Films

A person can get rich in the film industry, and they can just as easily go broke. Movies are a multibillion-dollar business with great risks and even greater rewards. When you're talking about money of this magnitude, the numbers really do matter.

It Pays to Act

The highest-paid actors today draw unbelievable paychecks. Mark Wahlberg starred in the films *Daddy's Home* (2015), *Daddy's Home 2* (2017), and *Transformers: The Last Knight* (2017). In 2017, he reached the number-one spot among actors by earning over $68 million. Overseas actors aren't doing badly, either.

Paparazzi are people who sell photographs of high-profile people, like actors.

Indian superstar and eight-time Filmfare Awards winner Shah Rukh Khan earned over $38 million in 2017.

The Price of a Blockbuster

One of the biggest challenges for a filmmaker is getting someone to invest the money necessary for production. *Avatar* (2009) cost over $700 million to make. But it earned its money back, making over $2.7 billion worldwide. The blockbuster *Pirates of the Caribbean: On Stranger Tides* (2011) was a little cheaper to make, with a budget of about $410 million.

The 4DX in South Korea is the world's first 4D movie theater. It includes smell, movement, wind, and water effects.

But it was another hit, making over $1 billion worldwide. However, not all movies make their money back. *Speed Racer* (2008) lost about $27 million, despite having an excellent cast, director, and production team. Critics blame the story line for this massive flop.

Bringing Back Moviegoers

Going to the movies is among the least-expensive ways to have fun. A family of four will spend about $35 for tickets to see a regular movie. If that family wanted to see a movie in IMAX or 3D, it would cost $15 to $20 a ticket. But that's still less than what

Many of Hollywood's filmmakers are committing to buy a set amount of Kodak's motion picture film in order to help the company compete against the digital age.

Regal Entertainment Group is one of the largest movie chains, with over 7,300 movie screens in 564 theaters in the United States.

Taking Informed Action

One way a movie company gets people into the theater is to create **trailers** that promote a new movie. Trailers are shown on television, on the Internet, and before the start of another movie. These give a little glimpse into a movie by showing a few scenes. However, trailers can sometimes give a misleading impression of what the film is about. Sometimes they even ruin the movie by showing all the important scenes. Have you gone to see a movie because you liked the trailer? If so, do you think the trailer helped or hurt the movie? The next time you watch a movie in the theater, think about what made you want to watch the movie.

tickets to a baseball game or theme park cost. That same family would spend about $165 for baseball tickets and about $360 to enter a theme park!

As cheap as movie tickets are today, they were once cheaper. Over the past 10 years, the average price for a movie ticket has increased 25 percent. This price increase is partially because of what movie theaters are doing to pull people back into the theater. Studies indicate that more people are staying home and streaming movies online from services like Netflix, Hulu, and Amazon Prime Video. Fewer people are actually going to movie theaters. Because of this, many theaters are now offering things like luxury seating, full-service dining, and the ability to reserve seats ahead of time.

Communicating Conclusions

Before reading this book, did you know about the movie industry? Now that you know more, why do you think it's important to know about the industry and how movies are made? What new developments in technology do you think filmmakers will use next? Share your thoughts with your friends and family, and ask them what they think.

Think About It

Monsters University (2013), produced by Pixar, required more than 100 million hours of computer time to create. In many cases, a single frame took as long as 29 hours and at least 24 frames were required for each *second* of the finished movie. A team of 270 people worked on the animated movie, yet it still took 4 years to complete. According to Kori Rae, the producer, this was actually a short amount of time. *Brave* (2012) took about 6 years to complete! On average, Pixar movies take 4 to 7 years to produce. Why do you think it takes so long to complete an animated movie? Use the information in this book and the research you find online and in your local library to support your answer.

For More Information

Further Reading

Buckley, Annie. *Making Movies*. Chanhassen, MN: Child's World, 2007.

O'Neill, Joseph. *Movie Director*. Ann Arbor, MI: Cherry Lake Publishing, 2010.

Willoughby, Nick. *Digital Filmmaking for Kids for Dummies*. Hoboken, NJ: John Wiley & Sons, 2015.

Websites

Kids' Vid
http://kidsvid.4teachers.org
Learn more about how to make a movie, from writing the script to editing the film.

PBS—Youth Filmmaking Programs
www.pbs.org/pov/filmmakers/resources/youth-filmmaking-programs.php
Find an organization or program near you to learn more about how to make films.

Whyzz—How Are Movies Made?
www.whyzz.com/how-are-movies-made
Find out more about the process of filmmaking.

GLOSSARY

blockbusters (BLAHK-bus-turz) nickname for movies that have higher-than-average success

box office (BAHKS AW-fis) the place in a theater where money is collected from those coming to see a movie

computer-generated imagery (kuhm-PYOO-tur JEN-uh-rate-id IM-ij-ree) images created through computers that make special effects in movies

dialogue (DYE-uh-lawg) the spoken parts of a movie

directors (duh-REK-turz) the people who oversee all aspects of the making of a movie, particularly the shoot

distributors (dih-STRIB-yuh-turz) companies that deliver films to movie theaters

documentaries (dahk-yuh-MEN-tur-eez) movies that present actual events or facts about something

dub (DUHB) to make a new recording of dialogue for a film that will replace the original

incentives (in-SEN-tivz) actions taken to try and persuade or inspire someone to make a certain decision

location scouts (loh-KAY-shuhn SKOUTS) people who travel to find ideal places for a movie to be filmed

marketing campaign (MAHR-ki-ting kam-PAYN) a defined series of activities used in promoting and selling products or services

media (ME-dee-uh) a method of communication between people, such as a newspaper

political propaganda (puh-LIT-ih-kuhl prop-uh-GAN-duh) movies or documentaries that try to convince viewers of a certain political point or influence their opinions; these movies show only one point of view

producer (pruh-DOOS-ur) a person, company, or area that oversees all financial aspects of a film

profitable (PRAH-fih-tuh-buhl) earning more money than it cost to make

revenue (REV-uh-noo) the amount of money that is made from some investment

screenwriters (SKREEN-rite-urz) people responsible for writing a movie's script, which will mostly be the dialogue for the actors

script (SKRIPT) the written text of a movie or other show

shoot (SHOOT) the actual filming of a movie

sound track (SOUND TRAK) the musical score of a movie

special effects (SPESH-uhl ih-FEKTS) images or sounds added to a movie by computer technology

storyboarding (STOR-ee-bor-ding) the practice of creating artwork in order to place and explain, scene by scene, how a film will be shot

studio (STOO-dee-oh) the name for the buildings and the land owned by a single company for the purpose of making movies

Technicolor (TEK-nih-kuhl-er) a process for making movies in color

technological (tek-nuh-LAJ-ih-kuhl) using knowledge from science and engineering to invent new devices or tools

top-grossing (TAHP-GROHS-ing) used to describe a movie that earns more money than any other movie

trailers (TRAY-lurz) short clips that give people an idea of what movies will be like

INDEX

blockbuster, 4, 8, 17, 25

Bollywood, 14, 15

camera, 5

computer-generated images (CGI), 11, 23

film(s), 5–8, 12, 13, 14, 17, 19, 21–24, 27
 animated, 8, 30
filmmaker(s), 11, 12, 14, 21, 23, 25, 27, 29
filmmaking, 17

Hollywood, 6, 8, 12–14, 17, 21, 27

Kinetograph, 5

political propaganda, 13

special effects, 11, 22, 23

technology, 5–7, 22, 23, 29
 Technicolor, 6

theater(s), 5, 9, 23, 26, 28, 29

United States, 5, 6, 12–14, 17–18, 21, 28